UNEARTHED

POEMS THAT UNEARTH

Also by Pushpa R. Menon

ORANGE: Elfchen Poems (2025)

Pushpanjali: A Collection of Poems (2024)

Lore and More: Narratives of Kerala (2024)

UNEARTHED

POEMS THAT UNEARTH

PUSHPA R. MENON

Published by Cogitabund LLP, India
publishing@cogitabund.com
www.cogitabund.com

UNEARTHED: Poems that Unearth

A Cogitabund Book/ published by arrangement with the author

ISBN: 978-93-49383-71-5

Typeset and Cover Design by Cogitabund LLP

Contents

Dedicated

To Jayaprakash who built more than walls to shape a home
around trees
and create a green space for my words to breathe.

Foreword

Earth Feast

Unearthed Poems

Pushpa Menon

What attracts us to the poems are its hueful blends and the rich observations from nature, its flora and fauna. Then, there's a poet whose heart with pleasure fills and dances. The book of poems with its hundreds of flowers, the green grass, birds, raindrops like memory's touch, the snakes, the eco worms, goldfish, the fireflies, the millipedes, seemingly so innocent, gains in meditative thought and poetic stature, such that the book of poems becomes an Earth Feast. An ecstatic wildness pervades. So does an accompanying tameness. There's an enchanted poet here walking through the woods. It is not just imagination. It is truth.

The poem 'Blueprint' is a thanksgiving to the one who

has made all this freedom of flora and fauna possible for the poet.

In the midst of such an Earth Feast is also the poet's awareness of reality that there lies hidden

'*In dank corners, in murky spaces, / dirt, cobwebs, dried insects' corpses /For eons unmoved, they silently sit, /Like dark skeletons in dismal cupboards hid.* (Camouflage)

Pushpa Menon's poetry is a clear stream. It is eloquent with simple natural beauty, and the reader is under no uneasy strain to interpret. Often, they are truthful fables of nature's lessons in endurance, or piety. In 'Coral Queen', love is a heavy price to pay, if one's love is blind.

Pushpa Menon's heart lies with nature, its flowers and rubbles as a nature poet's heart should. Here's a poet in her world of tear cups and buttercups. She is at home with eco worms, foraging millipedes, snake glides, and where *'yellow and blue butterflies in brocade wings/ adorn the purple fringe of the dying dusk / Rightfully rest in the honeyed cusp, / Of buttercup petals folded in maternal bliss. (*Dances in the Rain)'.

Pushpa wonders whether *'tear cups can hold the rain*

unshed' in them without yielding to a fall (Crimson Rains).

One of the most interesting poems is 'Detritivores' which resets our common thinking of beauty and of making love. It further makes us shudder at its sad and violent ending, though that love making never intended any harm. The poem is a pointer to how as humans we are careless to our eco system. The poem, a statement of innocent love, and the manner in which the love act is crushed by a passing car tyre remains poignant in the reading mind. Only a poet- heart, the kind that is hers, can render such touching verse.

'They envied none / His myriad mythical legs over her wrapped. / In proud disdain, oblivious, they quietly crept. / A car raced through in maddening daze. / Under cruel black wheels they were swept. / Not a whimper. Not a sigh. /Only the wind rustled by. / I stood aghast. / Ashamed.'

(Detritivores)

Pushpa's love for her dead pet is unforgettably etched in the poem ' Dog Years'

In heavy moments dark, / I hear your winsome bark. // In life's quiet lonesome path, / Tiny paw prints warm my heart.

Indeed, this is a garden book of flora and fauna of all kinds, in sunshine and rain that provide Pushpa Menon with her poetic inspiration and enhance or help sustain her poetic abilities. Added, the poems provide lessons in empathy, compassion, and earth bonding, without which one cannot claim to be a true poet.

While for most part there is peace in her garden, the poet is not blind or deaf to the doings of nature that can twist and torment the calm and peace as when she observes Kingfishers appearing in her pond

'They beat and turned the senseless prey, / Dragged it down the long, dark- tunneled way. / Predator and prey locked in fatal embrace –/ I *understood anew Nature's looped grace. I stood riveted as the kingfishers/ Glibly with my goldfish glided away.*

(Halcyon Days)

There are poems of introspection on the ascent, chasing slippery dreams as when the poet laments

In the mad rush to gather the fickle stars, / Why did we forget the moon was ours?

(The Lost Moon)

The poem 'More and More,' is one that brings the essential Pushpa to the fore, shed of anything ornate, or, frills or decor. It shows her ability to utter candid truths without a philosophic ache.

More and more I know, / How less and less I trust in love. / More and more I know, / How less and less the lights shine low. / If this be growth then, / More and more I know, / How less and less I want to grow.

The poem 'Silence' has the attractive line

Love, my love has a strange equation

And she amplifies it in a beautiful, sensitive way when she says

In the end I have only me to blame. / Love seeks not. Never tarries. Does not stray. / A part of me I once thought you loved, / Will forever in bliss, silently pray, / In hope, in strength young you will stay.

Unearthed, the poems, have a shine, a glitter as of those awakened from under-earth slumber, over which a little earth sprinkled, is growth, fecundity, and enviable poetic inspiration.

Gopikrishnan Kottoor

Preface

Poetry, for me has always been an act of quiet witnessing of the world within and the world without. It is a space where I listen to the whispers of leaves, the tremors of memory, the sighs of the forgotten, and the silences between words. Each poem in this collection emerges from such attentive moments which are sometimes luminous, sometimes unsettling but always honest.

Much of my writing is rooted in the natural world. Nature is not merely a setting but a companion, mirror, and metaphor. Rain, birds, soil, insects, and flowers are not passive symbols but active presences, echoing the rhythms and ruptures of human life. In their transience and tenacity, I find reflections of our own joys, struggles, and silences. Threads of womanhood — its strength, sorrow, endurance, and erasure — run quietly but insistently through many of these poems. Some verses honour unsung carers and mothers; others confront cruelty masked as custom or myth. I have tried to approach these themes not with bitterness, but with the steady gaze of truth and a compassion that refuses to romanticise suffering. Some poems speak of trees, of gods, of grief. Some draw inspiration from poets. In *Garden Greetings* there is an echo of Browning's "God's in His heaven—All's right with the world" from *Pippa Passes*. *Nevermore* is reminiscent of Poe's poem *The Raven*. The emotional landscape of longing, loss, ageing, love, injustice, wonder is deeply personal, yet I hope they echo shared human experiences. The poem *Carer Still at 89* is a tribute to the courage of a mother, an epitome of feminine fortitude and care. *The Last Breath* mourns the loss of a loved sibling. *Silent Sighs* grieves the death of a pet dog. The poem *Blueprint* is a thank-you sung in verse to my husband for the spectacular house that he built.

My aim is not to offer answers, but to hold space for reflection, empathy, and connection. If these poems stir a memory, a thought, or simply a moment of stillness in the readers, they have found their purpose. This collection brings together poems written over many years — some tender, some fierce, all born from an urge to observe, remember, and imagine a gentler, more attentive world. I offer them with gratitude and humility.

UNEARTHED

POEMS THAT UNEARTH

Ageing

A faded furrow.

A frayed rainbow.

Fires out blown.

Lines undrawn.

Circles bygone.

Love out worn.

A longing for home.

A pining forlorn.

A life run… undone.

Pink to purple the sun sinks stealthily.

Time tweaks, greying shades at sixty.

Blueprint

The terrain was red- brown, angry, hard.

A lone tree stood desolate in the yard.

He used no sickle, no sword, no knife.

Only his gentle sight, his sharpest insight.

To prise open the hard, unyielding land.

The green spread under his magical hand.

He drew no line between trees and wall.

Made room for light, breeze, summer and fall.

Windows wide for whispers, wind and wings.

Pools for fish to glide and flowers that sing.

Space for myriad creatures to flourish and grow.

For roots to spread and words to freely flow.

With bricks and dreams, he built our home.

A green blueprint etched in breath and stone.

Camouflage

Big mansions appear stately, spotless clean.

The dust deftly swept under the carpets unseen.

In dank corners, in murky spaces,

Dirt, cobwebs, dried insects' corpses.

For eons unmoved, they silently sit,

Like dark skeletons in dismal cupboards hid.

Carer Still at 89

Bent with age, as frail as can be.

Her skin sags under the weight of care,

Her bones brittle under constant repair.

Her gait is cautious, she smiles fleetingly.

She keeps vigil of her sick mate all night.

Nurses him through thick and thin.

Feeds him nasally, her eyes over brimmed,

Soothes his spirit with feigned delight.

Her world trembled, her courage swayed,

When malignancy snuffed his fragile spark.

He slipped quickly, quietly into the dark.

She wept once. Bowed. Silently prayed.

Her Sun had set, long shadows cast.
She sank, lost in the abyss of despair.
Her tired hands found yet another to care.
Her sibling long lost to a neglected past.

At 89 with her strength ebbing low.
Her eyes growing dim, gums sans teeth.
She works tirelessly like the proverbial bee.
Stressed, over strained, drained hollow.

She nurses, bathes, dresses, feeds her kin.
Some days her brows arched in a frown.
She cajoles, chides, comes heavily down.
Some days smiling a song, sporting a grin.

Her artless heart selflessly beats in care.

Across shiny weather or pouring rain,

Stumbling, phoenix like she rises again.

Enduring grace like hers, comes but rare.

Such small wonders make life sublime.

She is a priceless woman – my dear mother.

These lines I pen, are a song I sing for her,

To love. To cherish her fortitude feminine.

Coral Queen

I picked her up tenderly

Pallid petals on the ground upturned.

Her orange heart held a sunny glow

Before the sun rose, a while ago.

Night Queen! My coral jasmine.

Like her sisters twisted in toxic time,

She fell into love's abyss wide,

A dark hole parading love, disguised.

A winsome mate, her beloved sun,

Fiercely hot, his shiny armour undone,

Eyed her from the cloudless blue,

Then stepped down his chariot new.

Enticed by her guileless charm,

Knowing well what fatal harm,

Would on the naïve maiden befall,

He reached her humble cottage wall.

One kiss on her lips glowing bright,

His molten flame licked her white,

Ecstatic the coral queen stood crushed,

Her sweetness like nectar overflowed.

Lost like many in her fragrant tribe,

She paid heavily for love gone blind,

A life consigned to burning desire,

To seething passion gone haywire.

But what aches like a broken tear

Is not the beauty, not the fear,

Not her daring to embrace the flame,

Not her ashes smeared in shame –

What hurts most in the ancient lore,

Is how sanctified her fall was of yore,

When her throes, her shattered sighs,

Silently screamed across humankind.

The fragile coral jasmine, is known to bloom at night and fall with the coming sun. This poem reflects on the mythic archetype of the woman consumed by love — radiant, devoted, but ultimately destroyed.

Crimson Rain

The sun shies away from my window,
Disappearing into folds of thick clouds.
The wind pulls my drapes aside,
Dislodging petals from dark green boughs.

Honey-drunk bees forget to laze on buttercups,
The air grows thick with murky, perfumed breath.
Birds sing from broken twigs with urgent cries,
Deafening with a thousand notes, barren hillsides.

A rainbow curves shyly across his cheek,
Its many hues merging in the prismed light.
Raindrops fall slow from the cusp of blue,
Wet tears wrenched from the crimsoned hue.

Are tear-cups enough to hold the heavy drops unshed?
Can pale pearls cradle, in empty shells, the dripping drops of red?

Dances in the Rain

Dully I watch the singing drops,

Silvery soft, like memory's touch.

Tan brown, the cows moo plaintively.

Love-lorn, the mynahs mate furtively.

Majestic golden snakes glide stealthily.

Carps in my pond gather greedily.

My frugal fare they devour hungrily.

Huge foraging millipedes curl up defensively.

These eco worms feed in my decayed drain

And dance in the feathery rain.

Coral jasmines empty fragrances silently.

Roses bloom in bold hues of red, pink and peach.

Jade green leaves shimmer in coy delight.

Whistling winds pass raucously by.

Yellow and blue butterflies in brocade wings,

Adorn the purple fringe of the dying dusk,

Rightfully rest in the honeyed cusp,

Of buttercup petals folded in maternal bliss.

Dawn unfolds in dew scented breath again

And dances in the lusty rain.

The winged tweets rend the air.

A melancholic dirge to the retreating light,

Nestles quiet in my mango groves.

Wind gently sways in peace-filled breath,

Sings a lullaby rocking me to blissful sleep.

Weaver ants retire to their leaf- spun homes

Resting on promises of the morrow.

Warblers stretch in their scented shades.

Trust rides abreast the verdant plain

And dances in the wind- swept rain.

My heart trembles in forbidden joy.

Misted tear cups hide terror spots, torn in red.

Ears burn with the shrieks of disasters that spit fire.

War-stench of greed, the maniac odours of the violent creed.

Tanker leaks, jubilant stampedes, boiler blasted screams.

My screen is mute, my conscience door slammed shut.

I mask my cowardly soul in optimism pseudo indeed.

My soul leaps like the bard's, as the rain arches in a splendid bow,

Laments our fallen, graceless state, our senseless pain,

Escapes and dances with the all cleansing rain.

Dawn

Year after year, the lamp of Vishu,
Throws its benign flame on my flowers and fruits.
The mirror doggedly reflects—
My black wavy hair now wispy grey,

Smooth cheekbones, rugged, deeply frayed
My eyes do not blink at the flames burning bright,
They are heavy with unspoken shades of grey.
The light licks away the dark knots of the passing night.

A dullness grazes, settles on my weary breast.
Yellow laburnums bask softly in the golden light.
A broken tusk of my god head looks down on me
Knuckled fingers I lock in prayer.

Parched lips fond words utter:
A pure breath of health, harmony, and joy,
For the myriad creatures that walk my path, they pray.
Your grace I plead for my loved ones too.

For those I lost to death; for dreams that froze.
Sleep shuns me. My eyes droop, heavy with care.
Wait I must for my light to lift the dark smoke
Coiling, curling, covering my cloud-swept sky.

Detritivores

Unthreatened, unharmed, unseen,

Gently massaging her black, gold sheen,

Soothing her with whispered nothings,

Amorous he mounts her burnished back.

Entwined beneath the coppice tree,

Cuddled in the moist bed of littered leaf,

Lost, locked in a coiled embrace,

They stretched on the muddy surface.

Butterflies flitted, birds chirped,

A crimson flower fell.

Sun rose shyly behind its clouded veil.

Wind tore the branches to peep through.

Snacking, napping on their litter bed,

These detritivores on fallen fare fed.

Not fast, nor flashy they curl under threat.

No creature envied them. They envied none.

His myriad mythical legs over her wrapped.

In proud disdain, oblivious, they quietly crept.

A car raced through in maddening daze.

Under cruel black wheels they were swept.

Not a whimper. Not a sigh.

Only the wind rustled by.

I stood aghast.

Ashamed.

Distance

Two silent pools,

Shimmered like pearls,

A drop fell. They cried,

An ocean till dried.

Only a bed of sand remains,

Where once no drop could hide.

Smiles and glass,

Bonded like twins,

Shatter when silently tapped,

On rough edges,

Creating distances that loop,

Into knots that bind.

Stifled heartbeats,

Throbbed like dull pain.

A sigh skipped. The heart broke.

A tiny twig snapped.

Only the dry carcass remained,

Where once life breathed.

Weary miles,

Stretched like sad sighs.

A step missed. They fell.

A distance measured.

The race was done.

Where once they danced as one.

Soft whispers,

Weave magic of warmth.

They scream hollow,

When bitter pills are swallowed,

Churning magic into misery,

Deep within.

Dog Years

Your soulful eyes, your furry warmth,

Your anguished sigh.

The gentle fall of your tranquil breath,

Your nerve racking pain.

Your tongue rolling, your open mouth.

Ears that cock to silky whispers soft.

Tail that weakly wags freezing cold.

Your barks whine in laboured beats.

Your eyes locked in mine mutely you left.

On my lap cradled in grief,

I let your tormented breath sleep.

Etching you in my memories deep.

Seldom spoken of but forever lived.

Wordless you exuded love, loyalty, light.

Protectiveness you wore like a second coat.

Watchful you were to the core.

In heavy moments dark,

I hear your winsome bark.

In life's quiet lonesome path,

Tiny paw prints warm my heart.

Earth Song

Morning beckons shyly bright.

Silvery sun peeps through my window light.

Summer scented breeze draws my drapes aside.

Swaying flowers flaunt their fragrances wide.

Singing birds with persistent urgency tweet.

Buzz of drunken bees. Millipedes silently creep.

Rat snakes in armour of gold amorous bold.

Roses blush. White jasmine buds wait to unfold.

Sleep drenched, my bleary eyes open slow.

Dark deep pools shimmering, aglow.

A lonely drop from my tear cups flows,

Dries salt flaked on the mounds below.

A sunshine lost, a tender leaf blown,

A fallen flower, a broken feather flown,

A bleeding heart, earth's cry forlorn.

Love's magic lost, shared dreams torn.

Jasmines wilt, rose petals bend low.

Bees drip. Honeyed cups drained hollow.

Hours like dull aches stretch tirelessly long.

A dull refrain of a sad oft sung song.

Emptiness

A bird hops tentative, trembling, unseen
On my garden window dressed in green.
I wait for the lost song against my silent wall,
Drapes with bated breath stand heavy like a pall.

Shaky sills of my heart stare empty, bewildered.
Sorrow sits silent, screams unheard.
A bird tweets a chime in the distant twigs,
The melody faraway tugs gently at my heart strings.

My green buds, shy, hesitant then boldly bloom.
Clouds gather quiet, persistent then fiercely fume.
Their rain cups brim, tumble into a million drops,
Like tears on sad cheeks streaming across.

The musical strains fall, fumble, steadily fade.

I sigh. My bird has flown to a greener glade.

Was it bird, a singing minstrel in the azure blue

Or my hemmed in soul that silently flew?

Fiery Feathers

A bird flutters, a feather falls, silent.

Its wings hold the memory of flight.

A woman's gaze hides her spark,

In shades of jasmine light and dark.

The earth weeps. Brittle branches break.

Rains refuse to carry her leaden weight.

Birds rise. And women like earth, demur.

Undaunted by the light that leaves a scar.

Feathers of fire drift and smoulder.

Making wings and gazes stronger.

Fireflies

A little uncouth fly lay still,

On my cold window sill.

Thinking it dead, I tried to sweep it away.

It did not budge, never strayed.

I poked, pricked, pierced with my safety pin,

To pry it loose from the steely rim.

It stirred a little but stayed the same,

Stubborn wedged-in all day.

Why wouldn't the uncouth thing fly away?

When darkness came the creature stirred,

Out of its exile slowly moved and flew away.

A little spark trailing along the way.

Lit in its amber light my curtains glowed.

My head in shame humbly bowed.

Uncouth fireflies have fiery hearts

To keep the gathering gloom at bay.

Floral Feast

A splurge of greens – jade, emerald, dark,

Mellowed, pale, pleasing verdant sheen.

Flowers prancing in myriad hues,

Orange, violet, pink, shades of blue,

Crimson, yellow, fiery red too.

Magenta clad *vaadamalli,* my floral queen.

Lilac periwinkles frolicking in the wind.

White candles wimpled in priestly sheen.

Frosted lilies pink and peach, peeping buttercups.

Dazzling coral jasmines, frangipanis on pearly greens.

Rose fringed, ivory, burgundy oleanders sublime.

Flamboyant orange, sunny, hibiscus in soft pastels.

Sober *nandiarvattoms,* enduring *nitya kalyanis.*

Nodding grace of *rajamallis*, vibrant *madhumalathis.*

Corymbs of ixora florets, scented jasmine unfurled.

Perfumed capsules of *chamelis* tinged in purple tone.

Heliconia of multiple makes, stiff euphorbia, silent adenia.

Coppices, hemipilia housing humming birds' tweet.

Clustered lantanas, morning glory waltzing in breeze.

Yellow allamandas, glossy orchids in velvety silk.

Roses with thorns – ruddy, cream, soft peach.

Scarlet, fiery jade blossoms; golden cascades rich.

Fair lilies swanning in the waters green.

Sterling, stunning *mukuttis* in brilliant gleam.

My flowers bloom crisp in the summery sky,

Sway in breeze singing songs of grace

Breathe scented elixir to soothe the soul

Lend comfort to limbs; delight to the eye.

Hands fold in prayer as the colours blend,

Like heaven's arch on a starry night.

Fresh and Juicy

Folds nectar-filled with sweetness drips.

Squirts luscious, succulent, delicious treats.

Fruits prickly, dotted, smooth and spiky,

Purple, golden, pitted, rugged brown.

Ruby lipped cherries, burnished blue berries

Rose apple, juicy pearls dripping honey.

Lumber jacks; winsome, burgundy grapes.

Chickoos syrupy bowls of sugary delight.

Tangy lemons, soft creamy custard apples,

Sour plums, miracle fruits and gooseberries;

Native, Chinese seedless guavas replete

Hairy fiery rambutans, jewelled, juicy pineapples.

Hardened nutmegs in violent histories wrought.

Mangoes royal, stately with a golden gleam.

Birds on them generously feed, bees drink deep,

Leaving no room for our insatiable greed

Garden Greetings

Light filtering through the leaves,

Raindrops licking the eaves.

Birds twittering on the trees,

Flowers blooming for the bees.

Fallen fruits from the guava tree,

Snakes promenading in silently.

Worms crawling through the grass,

A glow worm's breathing spark.

A smiling face, a grateful heart,

A poet's faith gently reclaimed,

God's in our garden,

All will be right with the world*

**The lines echo Browning's "God's in His heaven—All's right with the world" from Pippa Passes.*

Halcyon Days

On my water trough they came, in pairs of two,

These harbingers of opportunities new.

Plumage bold, of incandescent hue,

Borrowed from the boundless blue.

A belly fiery orange from the sun.

A dagger-like bill that pierces through.

A bird that left many a myth behind,

Of Princess Alcyone and Ceyx* combined.

Swooping from the waters' edge biding time,

They rose like lightning into the sky.

Pounced on a tadpole, a spider, a fish –

Held them in a vice-like grip.

They beat and turned the senseless prey,

Dragged it down the long, dark- tunnelled way.

Predator and prey locked in fatal embrace –

I understood anew Nature's looped grace.

I stood riveted as the kingfishers

Glibly with my goldfish glided away.

Calm returned to the rippling surface.

Ushering in my halcyon days.

**In Greek mythology, Alcyone and Ceyx were deeply in love. Ceyx was killed during a voyage when Zeus unleashed a fierce storm, causing his ship to sink. Alcyone or Halcyon rushed to the shore and threw herself into the rolling waves, seeking to join her love in death. Zeus transformed them both into halcyon birds, a type of kingfisher.*

Happiness

Trees grow their girth like mysteries carved in wood,

Mystic, majestic rings springing in breeze every year.

Nebulous, tremulous clouds wander in the bed,

Of silver, rose, smoky, lightning blue.

Butterflies flit round their favoured plants,

Drowsy, drugged, dreamy, hanging on slender boughs.

Flowers bloom brilliant in pretty pots, in petty plots,

Buoyant, bright, buxom, swinging on tender stalks.

Ants crawl tirelessly atop the mango trees,

Slow, steady, steadfast, in the mundane tasks.

Birds twitter chirpy on the orange groves

Flimsy, flippant, frail, flying on breeze tossed twigs.

Snails slither stealthily under fallen leaves,

Slimy, soft, satiny, leaving a shimmering trail.

My dog whines in lazy languor,

Wagging tail, velvety nose, wistful slumber.

Goldfish caresses, kisses the silvery blue

Chortles, crackles, chuckles, swimming in the sunlit flow.

Owls hoot piercing the darkened veil when day is done.

Fowls crow to herald the golden sun.

To love, to live like a fish, a tree, a snail, a flower

It takes so little to breathe peace in nature's bower!

Leaving Home

Homes fondly lived in, spread roots within.

Wrapped in memories hating to let go,

Houses grow on you like a second skin.

How precariously they cling to my wall,

A hundred sighs, a rush of forlorn tears,

Gushing hot, unwilling to fall.

Breaths run deep to stretch in miles,

Sit still on sills like morning dew,

On wet petals, with vapoury shines.

Silhouettes, shapes, smells, shadow lines,

Of distant eyes love-lit, like stars in quiet sky,

Flicker unseen in unshed tears, in silent sighs.

Run down plasters like ragged thought bits,
Whisper of love, like buds of summer blooms,
Blossomed, burgeoned, brimmed in ecstatic bliss.

Corners echo, stretched-out kisses on lingering lips.
Like strung jasmine, the smell of love's laughter,
Now lost, faded, withered in wanton winds.

Flailing arms of my wind-blown mango twigs,
Weep loss of loved ones, drenched in pain,
On my cheeks fog -like dampness sits.

No spray of loveliness in my garden room.
No butterfly flits. The birds forget to tweet.
No fragrance abides in its frozen bloom.

No bees to hum my doleful song.

Squirrels on tree trunks no longer upbeat.

No ants in the leaf nests throng.

The slanting sun shadows cast.

Moments fade in ruthless ways.

The rising moon blurs the past.

Memories pierce like pelting rain.

Shadows breathe, dreams droop asleep.

Laughter rides astride in soundless pain.

Love, let's seek warmth in soft whispers,

Unmindful of the stench of emptiness,

Left orphaned in dank, dark corridors.

Lost Moon

Disturbed by a disquieting dream,
Rest evaded me – I could not sleep.
I drew aside the curtains. The air still,
I saw his dear face lined, haggard, thin.
A price he paid to stay glued to the screen,
Oblivious of the bond we swore to keep.

My mirrored sleep reflected the shattered glass
Of umpteen promises, across kinds and cast.
Panting breathless up and down the town,
Chasing slippery dreams that let him down.
Not knowing how close to Heaven we climbed,
How sadly we lost our moon, so sublime,

In the mad rush to gather the fickle stars,

Why did we forget the moon was ours?

More and More

More and more I know.

How less and less I depend on you.

More and more I know,

How less and less I see things through.

More and more I know,

How less and less I count friends true.

More and more I know,

How less and less I matter to you.

More and more I know,

How less and less I believe in what I do.

More and more I know,

How less and less I trust in love.

More and more I know,

How less and less the lights shine low.

If this be growth then,

More and more I know,

How less and less I want to grow.

Nevermore

The flap of the heavy wings. Black bird -smell.

Scooped stench poop

Over my little head swoop.

Overwhelming.

The timeless bird. Beyond death. Immortal.

Brow beaten. Bowed. Bent.

Lurking shadows of the net.

Mobile tower mocks.

Nature power rocks.

Broadbands stretch.

Screeching screens consuming. Bold.

The sky shrinks. Stinks.

Narrow black bands dotted on blue.

Like smoke vanish from my view.

Hooded AI 5G hisses "Nevermore".

Machines rant, rage, rave, raze.

Crows smitten outdone. Ravens outrun.

Shapeshifters stare amazed.

Eco sitters stand dazed

Without a flirt or flutter

Silenced. Nothing further to utter.

Leave humans behind to suffer

Fiery-eyed fowls fringed in folklore

Fly away lamenting, "nevermore".

Peach Roses

See them grow with the warmest glow,

My roses coloured in coral peach.

Roses that blush pink in satiny silk,

Hold a quiet feminine grace.

The velvety rose that breathes fiery red,

Stands scarred in wars, steeped in dread.

The vestal whites in sacred flame stand alone,

Like priestly herons carved in stone.

The sun-baked yellows dance in rain,

Bees, birds, beasts cavort in lively games.

The cream ones come in thoughtful shades,

A benign charm blossoming in quiet pace.

Peach roses neither pink, never red ablaze

Strike a balance with their moderate hue.

Bloom for peace, in temperate place.

A rose for harmony, a healing grace.

Rain Drain

Sprouting seeds.

Suckling babes.

Singing flowers.

Splashing waves.

Sweating brows.

Soothing breeze.

Swaying winds.

Shimmering streams.

Sucking fissures.

Sweeping tides.

Sparkling eyes smiling in rain.

Darkening clouds.

Dazzling skies.

Drone less hives.

Dream less beats.

Despairing sights.

Dusty feet.

Dreadful deeds.

Dripping boughs.

Doleful leaves.

Dwindling greens.

Dauntless earth rumbling disdain.

Sabre-toothed Rain

Wearily I watch the stinging drops,

Razor-sharp they hurl like splintered stones.

Tan brown, the cows moo plaintively.

Love-lost, the mynah mourns disconsolately.

Murky brown, the snakes spit venomously.

Herons devour my credulous carps ravenously.

Huge foraging millipedes get cut up even when curled.

The eco-worms rot in the decayed drain,

Dissolves, merges with the falling rain.

Coral jasmines fall unclaimed, lustreless

Rose petals scatter hues of peach, pink and red

Green leaves yellowed with edges frayed.

Keening winds beat their breathless chests.

Yellow and blue butterflies with battered wings,
Droop on the purple fringe of the dying dusk,
The honeyed cusp of my buttercups
Bemoans its butterfly less plight.
Dawn yawns, breaks murky, listless again
Apathetic, frowns on the dampening rain.

The birds tweet a melancholic dirge,
Soaked feathers heavy in feeble flight.
Wind sweeps away the peace-filled breath,
Tolls the knell of the fitful, frenzied sleep.
In rain drenched mounds fire ants burrow,
Bereft of promises of the morrow.
Warblers screech at the onset of doom.

Disasters lurk in the diabolic, dusty plain.

Guns shriek in the blood drenched rain.

My heart trembles in unuttered fear.

Misted eyes hide terror spots, torn in red.

Ears turn deaf smitten with arms that spit fire.

The maniac snarl of violence, the stench of greed,

Tanker leaks, jubilant stampedes, boiler blasted screams.

Muted screens, conscience door sealed shut.

Cowards conned in pseudointellectual narratives.

Souls no longer lament our fallen, graceless state.

Nor see the splendid arch the rain weaves.

Steeped in thoughtless, senseless pain,

I sigh at the sneering, sabre-toothed rain.

Sanctum

I heard the bells first.

I climbed the broad stairway.

I smelled the wick sesame oil dipped.

Brass bells chimed like a million hearts.

Stone lamps flame-licked, sticky stark,

Lit, like eyes glowing in the dark.

Incense sticks with smoke trailing thin.

At a small doorway, I let myself in,

A smaller one opened to reveal,

My adored tusker God sitting still.

I paused awed with all that floral spread,

Silken brocade, jewel studded head.

Why I wondered with all this gold,

Did my God to the broken tusk hold?

All knowing, omnipotent, my guiding light,

Couldn't you have got a better one outright!

"Inclusivity" breathed my smug, studied self.

"Equality across gender and kind", said my mind.

"Plastic surgery" mused my rational pride,

Sensing science in the sculpted shrine.

Chasing such petulant thoughts away,

I walked right through the door way.

A vacant space.

Silence pervades.

Stillness invades.

My heart sways,

An inner sanctum exposed.

To live is to be alive

Beyond all our senses.

To breathe is to worship

Divinity in the air, everywhere.

I felt my stone God flap His fan-like ears.

Sans pride, sans shame I let go my grateful tears.

Silence

Why did I allow you to snatch the smile from my lips

To share the ripe sweetness of our kiss?

Why did I open for you my heart

To so furtively tear apart?

Why did I place my joy in your care

To lay open my wound so bare?

Why do I never cease to love you

To keep getting hurt black and blue?

Why do I lose myself over and again

To wet my eyes and give me pain?

Why yearn to dissolve your secret held tight

To tell me that it will never set itself, right?

Love, my love has a strange equation.

Hurt hurting defying sense, spurning reason,

Baffling, blind, breathless, bracing delusion,

Blood gushing, unleashed tears spent, risen.

Maybe that's how you play the game,

In the end I have only me to blame.

Love seeks not. Never tarries. Does not stray.

A part of me I once thought you loved,

Will forever in bliss, silently pray,

In hope, in strength young you will stay.

Silent Sighs

He lay buried in our rugged patch.

His fine silk coat covered in fine silk.

Latching his last lingering look,

Fondly onto my raging breast.

His satiny paws cradled in my trembling hands.

His love licked me in gasping breaths.

He knew I loved him to the hilt.

Our days of frolic with love were filled.

We clung together doggedly in the car.

"Eat, my love", I whispered in his dog ears.

He blinked. His tail wagged. He winced.

The vet said, "It is the fleas, the mites come again."

My tears unshed fell like gentle rain,

"Dogs abstain from food when in pain.

A shot and he will be fine again.

Zest for food he must regain."

I treated him with food he loved to eat.

Believed he would soon be fine.

He responded dog like to my stimuli,

Wagged his tail. Nestled closely by.

Gazed at me unblinking. Grateful.

Nibbled. Thoughtful. Spat bile.

A yellow mucus fell in a soft mound.

I worried if he will come around.

I rushed him to the vet. He cringed. He sulked.

The vet prescribed blood test to set my fears at rest.

They drew his blood, red, dark purple, black.

He did not wince, bravely held my eye.

The day wore tirelessly on, harsh, blank,

He slipped further into his dream state.

More awake than asleep like shadows that creep,

Staring with his half-shut eyes, feigning sleep.

Night, late in the night, the results came.

I saw red. My heart trembled, bled.

In the silent sighs of the failing light

I saw him drift into the eternal night,

Two pairs of eyes refusing to wink,
We lay together on the cold marbled floor.
His eyes two dark pools tranquil, quiet,
Mine pleading, praying, desperate, sore.

His feeble whimper convoluted with anguish.
We sat awake all night, the dark closing in.
My raging heart against his throbbing one.
My hand flailing on his head racked in pain.

I drove him to the vet. My faith depleting.
One hand clutched against his human heart,
Another he let me hold his tortured head.
His tongue lolling, his eyes never once faltering.

In swift, silent spasms my dog slipped quietly away.

In a little box neatly packed, like a bruise he lay,

In my humble patch watching me every day,

Beckoning me like echoes from far away.

I do not weep. We neither sniff nor touch.

His cold dark grave, my lonesome shade,

Swept in pain, with warmth we re live.

Those tender moments we miss so much.

Sleeping Alone

Sleeping alone, Sleep divorced they say,

I am beginning to like this personal space.

Umpteen myriad dreams I chase,

Million humans come face to face,

Fortified by memories of stories deep.

Why compete with the insidious screen?

Sleeping alone, Sleep divorced they say,

Feels like growing strong —Nature's way.

Sleep-scape

The sky in my sleep-scape

Dances green and dark blue

Dreams spark bizarre shadows

Hope looms large – then shrinks

It talks, laughs, sings and winks,

Like birds and mammals do.

The thunder comes, a jolt from the blue

I stand on a precarious cliff wall

Mountains bristling, about to fall.

The dream maker pushes – drops me

I totter, stumble … not quite

My sky opens, draws the curtains – dark blue

Light slips in to pull me through.

Snakes and Silence

(In memory of Uthra — brutally murdered by her husband, Sooraj Kumar, on 7 May 2020)

Not a herpetologist, just a self -trained handler,

A flat headed weapon with fragmented scales,

He bought to rob his disabled wife of her gold.

With food and toxic tales, the viper he fed,

Slipped it onto her stupor-dazed bed.

A child beside her soundly slept –

Neither knew how close the danger crept.

The reptile struck, withholding venom,

A feeble wound on the sleeping woman.

Outwitted, outraged, his plan toppled flat,

He turned to a deadlier, spectacled brand.

Bottled it eleven days – angry, underfed –

Unleashed the cobra on her unwary bed.

No child beside her soundly slept.

The hood rose, the spectacle marks shone,

One vicious strike, and he was gone.

Spent, her fragile body poisoned again,

Shuddered. Slid into an eternal silence.

Snapshots

A school campus teeming with noise,
She looks around, a little lost,
He sees her. Their eyes lock.

A restaurant. Food steaming hot,
Unappetising in her mouth gone dry,
She gets up and walks away.

A pearly beach. Waters gurgling deep,
He clicks her sand-drenched face,
Something shifts. She stands amazed.

A busy bus-stand. People jostling fast,
She turns. His eyes meet hers, unsure,
He simply says, "I thought of marrying you."

A quiet temple smelling of sandal incense,
Amidst friends and close family gathering,
They exchange their wedding rings.

A new home, the lamps shining,
She steps in. He follows the light,
Hopes on their faces sparkling bright.

A bond of love, committed for life,
Smiles alight they walk hand in hand,
Unfazed into the moon-blanched land.

Swords

Raise your words, not your voice.

It is rain that grows flowers, not thunder. -Rumi

Some words that fall,

Like mist in sun,

Dissolve a wall.

Some words that fall,

Like frozen pillars,

Raise a wall.

Some words that fall,

Like blowing winds,

Stand you tall.

Some words that fall,

Like shadows at noon,

Shrink you to sizes small.

Some words that fall,

Like toxic turf,

Come covered in grime n gall.

Some words that fall,

Like roads that fork,

Call you to take a call.

Some words that fall,

Like the ticking clock,

Wither pitiful, pallid, pall.

Some words that fall,

Like a musical beat,

Ignite or memories stall.

Some words that fall,

Like abandoned hope,

Are mere words, mean nothing at all.

Treacherous like sly swords, some fall

Strike, slash, slit, stab, sever.

Words! all for nothing at all.

The Last Breath

A subdued day in torrid July trudged slow.

She walked with shoulders drawn, dropped, shy.

The pavement breathed heat, the breeze sighed.

Vehicles rushed madly past her, the dust bellowing behind.

She lifted her weary eyelids to gaze atop her mango tree.

Its leaves swaying lightly in the not so still breeze.

A tiny mango blossom like a pale moon looked on in disdain.

A blank stretch ahead with human-like heads at the wheel.

Mad hours rush mad to meet the fleeting minutes.

Her legs strained to stretch in the confines of her room.

Not yet. The vehicles blast their boastful horns. She must wait.

Or else be crushed under their thoughtless weight.

She yearned the shiny green shade of her forlorn tree.

A tiny mango blossom like an unshed tear smiled in disdain.

A little island on a head laced with wisps of greying hair.

Stared silent at the mango greens. Eyes droop unseen.

Her eyes followed the stranger's careful familiar gait.

His brawny hand not wanting to let go her white wicket gate.

Cars braked, brawled in endless line. Her fragile chest heaved as if in pain.

Her tree beckoned. Wind whistled in the mottled barks wistfully.

A tiny mango blossom like an unheard melody sighed in disdain.

She inhaled deep. Whispered loud his well-loved name.

Hoping. Not once did he pause. Not once turn around.

She licked the salt of her tear, bent in self-conscious shame.

Crazed. Unmindful of the spanking horns,

She crossed the wilful wretched road. He merely walked on.

Away from the benign mango shade. Away from its scented breath.

A tiny mango blossom like a forgotten smile smirked in disdain.

Clutching her slippery hope, she ran, he shadowed past her, fast.

The wind carried his name bellowing from her slender throat.

He paused. An eon passed. He turned around. He saw her ruddy face,

Creased in smiles he loved so well. Her hand warm like the setting sun.

His firmly clasped in hers they walked couched in affable silence.

The mango tree rocked, rustled, wrapped them in her shaded grace,

A tiny blossom like a fleeting dream blinked in disdain.

He held her close. Moments clung like memories.

His sinewy arm stretched like band across her slender waist.

So much spilled. A lot left unsaid. Two souls entwined as one,

Could hardly speak. Nothing to be said. Moments hung in dream.

Years of waiting, of grieving, of reprieve purged clean.

The tree swayed, sparkled, soaked in glistening green.

A tiny mango blossom like tender breeze winked in disdain.

Amidst plans drawn, lists made, memories exchanged,

The mobile beeped, its bell rang shrill. His face fell.

He would leave. She knew like siblings know.

They held hands. His sinewy arms smelled of embraces deep.

Her lips pursed tight. Afraid words would spill. Eyes weep.

Her tree moved shadowy, dressed in dark black green.

A tiny blossom like a hidden secret sighed in disdain.

She sensed the shadow mirrored on his beloved face,

A lingering look etched his dark eyes. Never guessed

What lay beyond his glazed gaze locked so far away.

Then in December he called just before the year's end.

He promised to come. The phone crackled, went dead.

The tree shook in despondence. Yellow leaves shed silently.

Its tiny blossoms like passing shadows slept in disdain.

In the wintry silence of the night when Christmas slipped.

Winds heavy with winter fog, she woke from a fretful sleep.

The 'phone buzzed, merged with her dream doused state.

Wide awake when he answered at the first bell. Her call!

A female voice said in an unmistaken monotone, "He is dead."

His breath trapped in the mango tree, caressed his siblings three.

A tiny mango blossom like his mother's tear hung in eternal misery.

The Screen

Vast abysses of aloneness,

Yawn open-mouthed idly.

Rain sprays the pain washed face,

Merges with the ubiquitous tear,

Pours unseen, subdued, soft.

Where is the hand that can touch the soul?

Where the voice that can soothe a sore?

Where the eyes that can illumine the blur?

Where the heart that can calm the storm?

Where the mind that can open memory's door?

Senses go numb. Reason falls apart.

My hour glass empties swift and sullen

The screen shimmers slightly, silently, slyly.

A Shopping Mall

Humble road-side shops stand small.

They have things but not enough of all.

No self-service to brag or shout,

Just service quietly handed out.

Keepers perch on their stately stools.

Helpers on their heels run not by rules.

Goods are good, stock limited to a few.

Fare displayed on black boards in open view.

Smell of stationery, grocery, garments new,

Spices, scented oils, array of toiletries too.

Discussion on politics, cricket and rain,

A mix of health, business, losses and gain,

A place for a quick chat, a tea, a chirpy stop.

Relics of the dead past, this social spot.

Snarling traffic skids past the glittering mall.

Glass and gloss rise intimidating tall,

Elite crowds strut their stylish gear,

Brandish branded goods in noisy flair.

Fashion dudes with one another vie,

Sassy pants, hair in multi-textured dye,

Dazzles, glimmers, glitz and glamour,

Perfumes that drown all the natural odour.

Food that blazon health, beauty, power,

Artificial drinks with natural flavour.

Trolleys groan with surplus wares,

Lured by 'more for less' pseudo sales.

Where personal is political; political, cynical,

Derangement lurks beneath a shopping mall.

The Twin-tailed Bird

The twin-tailed black bird,

Flew in through my window,

Beckoning her, the mate too.

Seeing humans around, the male panicked,

Eyed his mate a moment, poised and out it flew.

She watched perplexed, hopped, hoped it wasn't true,

That out of the window he flew,

Not once looking back to his love so true.

She flitted, fluttered and flapped her wild wings

Chirped, nay, shrieked so loud,

Like a scream in a desperate dream,

Willing him to come back to her.

How could he not! But she knew,

That out of the window he flew

Never to return to his love so true.

Her movements went wild.

Her delicate wings,

Like the sail of a sinking ship feebly flapped.

Her bony head she beat against my window pane.

It had all but snapped.

I spoke to her in gentle tones.

Guided her to the open door.

She did not panic. She stood dazed, lost in thought.

Turned away from the open door.

The window shuddered with her fragile flutter.

Not wanting to break free. Unwilling to accept,

That out of the window he flew,

Never to return to his love so true.

Gently on my cat's paw, I slid the window open,

She paused, briefly met my eye.

"Kindred soul", I whispered. "Feel the air. Look at the azure blue.

Your wings are strong. Your heart profound. Forget, forgive,

That out of the window he flew,

Never to return to his love so true."

Her twin tiny blades of wings trembled ever so slight

Did she gasp when the light hit her little birdie face?

As out of the window she flew,

To return with strength anew.

Thrushes

Thrushes, warblers, coucals, mynahs,

Drongos, crows, ravens, kingfishers, herons,

Arachnids, reptiles, wasps in dreaded grey,

Slugs, worms, frogs their favoured prey,

Millipedes, centripedes, munching all the rot away.

My garden laced in innumerable shapes of leaves,

Huge, variegated striped, all kind venations combined.

Tiny leaves that shiver in the breeze,

Giant plantain leaves that invite a sumptuous feast.

Nature's dainties might and beauty spread,

Humans harp on guns, violence and dread.

On Vasant Panchami

Sun slips from its frozen cusp like ice,

Melts, flows from the frosted snow.

Sky bellows, clears its murky chest,

The shine on its face a soft languid flow.

Seeds peep shy from the sepulchred earth

Like caterpillars cocooned in glossy glow.

The Goddess descends in her chariot blue

Glazed burnished like amber gliding low.

A slightest frown, a tender scorn,

Like fuzzy smoke on her lustrous brow.

Her abode of love the river bed a muddy spread.

North- west, north or west? Just a wayward lore.

Her banks have shrunk, the stories waned. Magic spurned.

No legends of love, nor aquatic silky sheen any more.

The verdant green, the mustard bloom, the vibrant gold,

The river's surge, the learned seers, the fables spun in yore,

Hammer, hammock, harp, pen, sickle, sword,

Washed in floods of greed, guilt, in ghastly gore.

Saraswathi, powerless you stand. Are you my river queen?

I see you dance waltzing in your mighty stream.

Where is hidden the glory, the fury, the silvery gleam?

Like your sisters you cradled, breast fed civilisations doused in dream.

Spun stories that cease to cascade down parched throat, slipped unseen.

Streams dissipate, disappear in thoughtless pride.

Shy periwinkles peep from crevices forget to bloom.

Deserts appear to reign supreme stagger, shrink, die.

Trees shake their lumber heads to ward off the darkened gloom.

Mountains high, ocean's shore, the forest green in legends hide.

Gnarled roots entrapped in malicious machete's diabolic doom.

Goddess of love, we beheld you in your ponderous strength.

Worshipped at your dainty feet. Tugged at your lace-fringed hems.

Revered the pearly beads, sacred scroll, lotus perch, snowy swan.

Learnt skills of art, music, agronomy, of divine love galore.

Celebrated knowledge, prosperity, energy to create, to adore.

Initiated young minds to write, read, talk, nature's simple chore.

Oh, Goddess dear wherefore did we shun the whispers of heart, of soul?

Water nymph! goddess of love, wisdom enshrined!

Forsake not the waylaid hopelessly lost human kind.

Rush down the heady heavens of mountains sublime,

From your cavernous cove, down vaults of endless time.

Gush through our hearts hardened with greed, gall, grime.

Flow to purge our chambers with your elixir divine.

Teach us anew the power to love, to nurture all living kind.

Breathe in us love that transcends hatred, blurs boundary line.

Walls of Silence

Lovers, like masons also build a wall,

Scaffolded with Trust, Truth, tested in Time,

Firmly cemented with tears, dry blood, gall.

Till a tiny treacherous touch tears it apart,

Shrouding velvety dreams in sepulchred silence,

Weaving memories drenched in sighs across a barren heart.

My cold wall, grows steep, stripped, seamless, sad,

Fills no voids. Leaves tongue parched, eyes glazed, vacant,

Whispers no warmth. No song in shrill voices raised mad.

Gaping gaps of dreams left behind,

Like orphaned souls in fiery floods,

Hide stormy stories, the pain, the pride.

Promises made, unkept, broken, blind,

In blanketed silences lost, kept alive,

Screaming silent in the dead of night.

Hot tears tumble, in muffled pillows fall,

Trapped sighs long for reprieve, a release,

The walls only stand mute, stoned, tall.

Feral secrets, feigned solace buried deep within,

Faked courage, borrowed boldness, tears bravely held,

Whimper softly, where laughter once reigned supreme.

What Else is Shine

Your lustrous eyes like million stars in the sky

Make aglow my darkened nights.

Your rounded fists unfold like petals abloom

Hold in its cushioned cusp my unshed tears.

Your supple limbs entwine like jasmine twigs

To scatter fragrance on my dreary days.

Your loving heart beats music into my ears.

Pillows my weary care-worn head to rest.

Vaulted lips shut tight seal mine with a hundred kiss.

Their whispers like magic dance in joy.

The quiet curve of smile, silent gurgle of laughter.

Spread like wet mud the heady smell of petrichor.

Unspoken promises raining down on quivering buds,

Of roses satin like slumber on my sleep-drunk dreams.

Love satiated thirsts for more and more,

A hunger runs amok along a dusty shore.

Where have they flown

The trust, the light, the repose?

The sun flickers and fades like the evening stars,

My blue-sky dips burnished, angry red, dark.

Silent deep seeds entrenched in the slimy sand.

A choking by an unseen alien hand.

Light pierces my nights enshrouded in vain,

Knowing the shine will never be the same again.

Wheel Chair-Bound

She slipped when the world slept.

Supine on the hard floor, unable to rise.

No one heard the sighs on her withered lips.

Nor the smothered cry of her fragile heart.

Battered, bartered since her childhood days.

She lay unmoving in the still darkness.

Her stoic self, refused to cry or call.

Was it pride or refusal to wake them all?

Help came with the first rays of the dawn.

Her legs sprawled, her face contorted, drawn.

Gently she was lifted off the hard floor,

Placed on soft bed by the kind souls four.

Her right hip bone blazed a fiery red.

Her leg immobile on the white bed spread.

Her eyes glistened in loving gratitude,

Dauntless, fearless in stark solitude.

Corona raked its claws in malicious glee,

Shutting down hospitals thoughtlessly.

Yet a smile flickered on her wrinkled face,

She fought off pain in her usual grace.

Later X-ray revealed her fractured hip,

The bone healed but slipped,

Calcified off its socket cage,

Bearing with it the weight of age.

Old, shattered with none to call her own.

Spanning nine decades and a half alone,

She lives in resilience profound

Breathing strength, wheelchair-bound

www.ingramcontent.com/pod-product-compliance
Ingram Content Group UK Ltd.
Pitfield, Milton Keynes, MK11 3LW, UK
UKHW040556200726
13845UKWH00067B/420

9 789349 383715